D1530233

THE GHOST OF I

and Other Celebrity Spi

THE GHOST OF ELVIS

and Other Celebrity Spirits

DANIEL COHEN

G. P. PUTNAM'S SONS   NEW YORK

Copyright © 1994 by Daniel Cohen
All rights reserved. This book, or parts thereof,
may not be reproduced in any form without permission
in writing from the publisher.
G. P. Putnam's Sons, a division of The Putnam & Grosset Group,
200 Madison Avenue, New York, NY 10016.
G. P. Putnam's Sons, Reg. U.S. Pat. & Tm. Off.
Published simultaneously in Canada
Printed in the United States of America
Designed by Patrick Collins
Text set in Sabon

Library of Congress Cataloging-in-Publication Data
Cohen, Daniel, date. The ghost of Elvis / Daniel Cohen. p. cm.
1. Ghosts—Juvenile literature. 2. Celebrities—Miscellanea—Juvenile
literature. 3. Ghost stories—Juvenile literature. 4. Apparitions—
Juvenile literature. [1. Ghosts. 2. Celebrities—Miscellanea.] I. Title.
BF1461.C667 1994 133.1—dc20   93-38030 CIP AC
ISBN 0-399-22611-7

10 9 8 7 6 5 4 3 2 1

First Impression

To W.E.D.

Contents

THE GHOST OF ELVIS
and Other Celebrity Spirits

Death Styles of the Rich and Famous

I MAKE NO BONES or apologies about it—this is a celebrity ghost book. It's a name-droppers' ghost book, a gossip-column ghost book.

You will find no anonymous "grey ladies" gliding noiselessly up and down dusty corridors in these pages. There are no spirits of butlers or bus drivers here. Those who have encountered the ghosts are no ordinary folk either. This is not a very democratic book.

There are some kings of England and the King of rock 'n' roll. There are stars of stage, screen, and television, a couple of well-known writers, some fairly well-known assassins, a professional wrestler, a famous general, even Superman himself. This is a *Who's Who*, a

Debrett's Peerage, a *National Enquirer* of the spirit world.

You may notice that there are a number of celebrity spirits who have been left out. I have not covered the several headless queens of England who are said to haunt the Tower of London, or other places of execution. Nor have I gone over the many, many ghostly appearances attributed to President Abraham Lincoln. Aaron Burr, whose spirit has been spotted all over New York, isn't mentioned. I don't even discuss John Wayne's haunted yacht. The reason I have avoided these celebrated cases is quite simple. I have written of them elsewhere, and I have no desire to repeat myself.

I make no claim for the authenticity of any of these accounts. I mean I can't prove that Elvis Presley was hitchhiking outside of Memphis three years after he died. Nor can I prove that the drunken ghost of Edgar Allan Poe can be found staggering along the streets of Baltimore, where he died. I wouldn't even try. But these are tales that have been widely reported, and at least some people believe them. You may believe them or not—as you see fit. But since we are all to a greater or lesser degree celebrity watchers (even if we hate to admit it), and we all love strange and ghostly tales (if you didn't, you wouldn't have picked up this book in the first place), I trust that you will enjoy them.

CHAPTER ONE

The Ghost of Elvis

ON THE AFTERNOON of August 16, 1977, an emergency
call came into the Memphis Fire Department in Tennessee. Somebody was having difficulty breathing at 3764
Elvis Presley Boulevard. The paramedics who rushed to
the scene knew the address well. It was Graceland, home
of the singer for whom the street had been named. They
suspected the victim was Vernon Presley, Elvis's father,
who had already suffered one heart attack.

The suspicion was wrong. The victim was Elvis Presley himself. Elvis was rushed to Baptist Memorial Hospital, where doctors worked frantically over him for half
an hour. It was no use. The patient was declared dead

on arrival. The official cause of death was listed as a heart attack.

The King of rock 'n' roll was only forty-two years old. Though he was no longer truly at the height of his fame, he had millions of devoted fans throughout the world. Tons of flowers and tens of thousands of people arrived at Graceland. President Carter issued an official statement from the White House. The governor of Mississippi declared a day of mourning, and the governor of Tennessee had all the flags lowered to half-staff.

Elvis fans were saddened, shocked, and disbelieving at the news. And somehow, the rumor spread that Elvis wasn't really dead.

It wasn't as though Elvis had been "lost at sea" or had otherwise disappeared, and had been *presumed* dead. He died in his home. His body was properly identified by friends and relatives. No one close to him expressed the slightest doubt that he was dead. There were, and still are, legitimate questions about how he died. But there should be no question at all that he is indeed dead. And yet, almost immediately rumors began to circulate that something very strange was going on. It was said that the body on display in the coffin at Graceland didn't really look like Elvis, that it was in fact a wax dummy.

And then stories of Elvis "sightings" began. Elvis was "seen" working at a gas station in Alabama or shopping at a convenience mart in Michigan, buying a gift for his daughter, Lisa, at a craft fair in upstate New York, and in lots of other ordinary places. The idea which seemed to underlie so many of these reports was that Elvis, fed up with the pressures of fame, had faked his own death and had adopted a new identity, so he could lead a simpler life. A life not unlike that of the people who claim that they had seen him.

Another somewhat more bizarre theory is that Elvis had identified some big-time drug dealers who then swore to kill him. The government, or some private group, helped the singer fake his death and put him in some sort of witness-protection program. Someone actually wrote an entire book on this theory.

The stories of Elvis "sightings" didn't really begin in earnest until 1988, a full decade after the singer's death. There had been earlier reports, of course, but the one that really caught public attention came from Louise Welling of Vicksburg, Michigan, near Kalamazoo.

"I saw him in the grocery store this one Sunday in 1987. [It was months before reporters latched on to the story.] I remember really well. We had gone to church, and every Sunday I stop at the store for something or other. I thought it was really odd this one particular Sunday because no one was in there, not even a customer, or so I thought. Not even the girls at the check-out.

"Then I went and got my things, and when I walked up to the counter, there he was. I really believe I looked at Elvis Presley . . . I was kind of stunned. . . . He just smiled at my grandson, who was with me. Whatever he got, it sure wasn't groceries because I couldn't see anything big on the counter. Whatever it was, it must have been tiny. I thought it was a fuse or something. He didn't have a big bag of groceries or anything when he went out."

Mrs. Welling has taken a lot of ridicule because of her story, but she isn't backing down. "I don't care what they say. The more you tell the truth, the harder you tell the truth, it's got to pull through one of these days. It has to. I just know it. I'm not giving up." And ridicule or not, she is believed by many.

Why this particular and quite simple account caught on, while more dramatic and more interesting stories did not, is impossible to know.

Stories of this type tend to pop up after the death of any prominent person, particularly if that person died young. But in the case of Elvis, the excitement has been extraordinary and really unprecedented. The rumors were fed and spread by the sensationalist tabloids sold primarily at supermarket checkout counters. Astonishingly enough, a lot of people seemed to actually believe what they read. "If it wasn't true they couldn't print it," people often say. A nationwide poll taken not too long ago indicated that nearly ten percent of the people in the United States believed that Elvis was still alive, and hiding out somewhere. And the sightings continue, indeed they may be increasing. It is all quite astonishing.

While those of us who recount ghostly tales often ask our readers to suspend their disbelief for a time, this is going too far. Elvis Presley died on August 16, 1977. Anyone who sees him walking around today is probably seeing one of the ever-expanding army of Elvis imitators, or something else.

An awful lot of people have said that they have had some sort of "psychic vision" of Elvis, or have actually seen the dead star's ghost. These accounts intrigued psychiatrist Dr. Raymond A. Moody, Jr. In 1975 Dr. Moody had written a book called *Life After Life*. It was about what he called "near-death experiences," people who "died"—that is, stopped breathing—and who were then "brought back to life" by a variety of medical techniques. According to Dr. Moody, many of these people reported strange, yet similar experiences while they were "dead." His book was a bestseller, and Dr. Moody himself became quite well-known. So it was natural that people would report strange experiences to him, including several involving Elvis Presley. He gathered them together in a truly fascinating little book called *Elvis After Life*. Here are a couple of the stories that Dr. Moody was told.

On December 20, 1980, a truck driver named Jack Matthews was hauling a load from out West to Memphis. After unloading in Memphis, he planned to drive to his home in Alabama for Christmas. Jack was in a hurry, for his mother had been ill, and he wanted to make sure that he was home for her birthday, which was on the twenty-first.

About a hundred miles outside of Memphis, Jack stopped for fuel. He was walking around the outside of his truck to stretch his legs, when he saw the figure of a man carrying a bundle under his arm emerge from the bushes across the road from the station.

It was dark and the man was wearing an overcoat and a big hat, so Jack could not see him clearly. But he felt sorry for the fellow and walked across the road to talk to him. He asked the man where he was headed and the man said Memphis to see his "momma and daddy" for the holidays. He had a Tennessee accent and a deep voice. He said he was going over to the highway to hitch a ride.

Jack didn't like to pick up hitchhikers. He had once picked up a man who pulled a knife on him, and since that time he hadn't trusted anyone. He didn't intend to give this fellow a ride either, no matter how sorry he felt for him. But after he got back in his truck and went about a quarter of a mile, he saw the man with the bundle walking along the highway, and almost without knowing what he was doing, he stopped and offered him a ride to Memphis.

The ride was pleasant enough. The hitchhiker was very polite, and it turned out that he and Jack had several interests in common. As they chatted about cars, a subject that fascinated both of them, the hitchhiker mentioned that he owned several Cadillacs. Jack figured he was just a poor boy trying to sound big. Why would a man who owned several Cadillacs be hitchhiking the week before Christmas? But he kept his doubts to himself.

As the truck drew near Memphis there were more lights on the road, and Jack was able to get a better look at his passenger. The fellow looked familiar, though he still couldn't see him very well. The passenger said that he wanted to go to an address on Elvis Presley Boulevard in Memphis, and Jack said that he would drop him off somewhere close by.

Then ride was almost over when Jack realized that he had never introduced himself. "My name is Jack Matthews," he said, and glanced over at the hitchhiker.

The man looked straight at him and said, "I'm Elvis Presley, sir."

Jack was stunned, and said something like, "You've got to be kidding." But he knew the passenger wasn't kidding, and the more he looked at the man the more he realized that he *was* Elvis Presley.

By the time the hitchhiker got out, Jack was shaking badly and barely able to control his truck.

Jack had never particularly been an Elvis Presley fan, and had certainly never visited Graceland. But two weeks after his encounter he got up enough courage to pay Elvis's home a visit. He found that it was very near the spot where he had dropped off the hitchhiker.

Was Jack Matthews making the story up? Did he have

an hallucination or dream? There is no way of knowing. Or, "Maybe you really did see the ghost of Elvis Presley," Dr. Moody told him.

Janice McMichael had known Elvis briefly during the early 1970s, when she had been trying to work in the entertainment business. Elvis knew many people and Janice never claimed that her friendship had been anything special, "though I certainly had my own fantasies."

The last time they met was in 1975. Janice had just arrived from Southern California into a cold and rainy climate. She wasn't adequately dressed, so Elvis gave her a light tan jacket. He was always giving things away, and never asked for them back. She regarded it as a special and cherished present. She put it in a plastic bag and hung it in her closet.

Then, shortly after Elvis died, the jacket began acting up! Janice would go off to work, and when she returned, she would find that the jacket had fallen to the floor. For over two years it had hung quietly in the closet and had never fallen. Janice took it out of the plastic bag, hoping that would help. It didn't. Once the jacket slid right off the hanger while Janice was looking at it.

The scariest experience came on the night of November 20, 1977: Janice awoke in the middle of the night and glanced over at the closet. There was a night-light in the hall which illuminated the side of the closet on which

Elvis's jacket hung. She watched in fascination and horror as the right sleeve of the jacket moved slowly up and down. This may have gone on for as long as half an hour.

These incidents badly frightened Janice, though she never considered giving up the treasured jacket. But for the first time in her life she got a roommate, a young woman named Mary. Mary had a pet miniature collie named Sparky. While Janice never told Mary about the jacket, Sparky seemed to know something. He would spend hours barking at the closet. Then after a few weeks his behavior changed. He wouldn't go near the closet. He acted as if he were afraid of it.

"Janice, what do you have in that closet?" Mary once asked. "Sparky thinks there is something in there."

Unnerved, Mary moved out after a few months.

Activity around the jacket gradually faded. There was only one more really notable incident. One night, Janice slid the jacket over to make room for other clothes on the rack. When she touched the collar it was wet. All of the other clothes in the closet were perfectly dry.

Polly Tyson was a great Elvis fan, and had been since she was nineteen years old. Like so many Elvis Presley fans, Polly felt a deep personal identification with the entertainer, though she had never met him. She was very upset and depressed by the news of his death.

Polly and her best friend, Doris Taylor, also an Elvis

devotee, spent a lot of time in Polly's kitchen drinking coffee and talking about Elvis. On the singer's birthday, the first since his death, Polly and Doris sat in the kitchen eating banana splits and Dreamsicles, two of Elvis's favorites, and playing his records. Three or four days later the two women were back in the kitchen at their usual spots. From where Doris was sitting, she had a full view of the solid-walnut pantry door.

"I looked across the table at Doris, and she looked white as a ghost. She was staring at the door.

"She said, 'Polly, I see Elvis's face on your pantry door.' "

And there it was, the familiar head and shoulders of Elvis, made from the pattern of lines and swirls in the grain of the wood.

The house had been built in the 1870s and as far as Polly knew, the door had been part of the original structure. In any event it had been there as long as she had lived in the house, and though she had looked at the door thousands of times, she had never seen this particular pattern before, nor had anyone else. Yet now it was obvious. When Dr. Moody was taken in to look at it, he said, "The image itself seemed almost to float a minute distance in front of the surface of the wood, almost as though one could see the door *through* the image."

Where it had come from, and exactly when, no one could say.

◆　◆　◆

The Ghost of Elvis

An elderly Tennessee farmer named Claude Buchanon told Dr. Moody of the curious way he found out Elvis had died. The farmer had known Elvis slightly. The singer had visited his farm a couple of times, and even slipped him some money when he was in financial trouble. Everyone says Elvis was like that.

One day Buchanon was out in the field behind his house, tending to a cow that had been injured. He looked up to see Elvis walking up the hill toward him. "He looked the same as he always did, except at first there was what looked like blue smoke or fog around him, just slight."

The farmer was very surprised. He didn't know why Elvis had come or how he had gotten around back without being seen driving up the road.

"What are you doing here, boy?" he shouted.

The figure was then about ten feet away, and Buchanon could see he was smiling. He said, "I've come to say good-bye for a while, Claude."

At that moment the farmer saw the screen door of his house fly open, and his wife, Thelma, run across the yard. He first thought the kitchen must be on fire because she was running so fast. She was shouting something, though he couldn't make it out. But as she got closer he heard her saying, "Elvis has died! It's on the radio."

Buchanon was stunned. He looked around for Elvis, but the figure had disappeared.

The farmer added, "I've never believed in these things."

Anyone who has spent time studying ghostly events will find these accounts familiar—dare I say hauntingly familiar? All sorts of ghostly hitchhikers have been reported throughout America. Objects associated with a dead person have frequently been seen to move mysteriously. Even phantom faces suddenly appearing on a wall or a floor are well-known. And what is called the "crisis apparition," the sudden appearance of an image of a person who has just died, or is near death, is one of the most frequently reported of all psychic experiences. What makes these particular accounts unique is that they have all been associated with one particular celebrity—Elvis Presley, the King of rock 'n' roll.

So the next time you see that heavyset guy with the long sideburns, pumping gas at the local service station—take a good, hard look. You never know!

CHAPTER TWO

Royal Ghosts

TODAY, A DIVORCE in the royal family of England is given front-page coverage in newspapers all over the world. It may even be the basis for a TV miniseries or two. It's something we common folk gossip about, but a few centuries ago royal divorces were a very serious business. They were often finalized with the words, "Off with her head." As a result the headless ghosts of several queens have been seen wandering the corridors of ancient castles or towers.

Simply disagreeing with the king or queen could result in a forced meeting with the headsman. And so the castles and towers are also the home for the spirits of losing candidates for the throne, unsuccessful rebels, disgraced courtiers, royal favorites who fell from favor, and so forth.

It's been a long time since Britain's royal family has been able to get rid of its problems with such blood-thirsty efficiency. Rather than being sent on a one-way trip to the Tower of London, troublesome family members and others are more likely to go straight to the tabloid press. One suspects that today's royalty becomes a bit nostalgic for the good old days, when personal disagreements were swiftly and permanently dealt with.

Given their history, it is hardly surprising that some members of the British royal family still retain an interest in the subject of ghosts. Prince Charles's fascination with what might be called the paranormal is well-known.

The current royal family of England is now called the House of Windsor. However, they originally came from the little German duchy of Hanover. The first of the line, appropriately enough George I, was brought over to England in 1714 as sort of a compromise candidate. He was a steady, not very ambitious man, who could be counted on to stay out of the way of the powerful politicians who were really running the country. He wasn't likely to try to have anybody beheaded either. The day for that sort of activity had passed. George I didn't like England very much, never really learned the language, and spent as much time as possible back in Hanover.

His son George II didn't like England either. And the

English public didn't like him. The public suspected, quite correctly, that the king favored the interests of Hanover over those of England. George II spent his final years in Kensington Palace, waiting for mail from "home," that is, Hanover. He was forever glancing up at a curious old weathervane high up over the main entrance to the palace, hoping for winds that would bring ships, and thus news from Germany. Today, when there are strong winds blowing, the grey face of the king is reportedly seen, still gazing up at that weathervane from the window of the room in which he died.

Princess Margaret, sister of the current queen, lived at Kensington Palace for years. She was once asked if she had ever seen the ghost of George II. "I'm afraid not, but I live in hope," she said.

George III is remembered in the United States as the tyrant who drove the colonies to revolt. He is remembered more fondly in England. At least he learned to speak the language tolerably well, and he was around for a long time. He reigned from 1760 until his death in 1820. By the final years of his reign, however, he had become totally mad, and was confined to Windsor Castle.

Practically the mad king's only amusement in those final years was gazing out the window of his chamber to watch the parade of the horse guards. Occasionally, he would wave feebly at the captain of the guard. A few days after the old king's death, the captain of the guard glanced up at the window, and saw the familiar figure waving at him. It was a most unnerving experience.

But a better-known ghostly appearance is that of the confused old king wandering aimlessly through the halls of the castle muttering "What? What?" as he often did while he was alive.

The next king, George IV, had spent many years as regent for his incompetent father. To history, he is better known as the Prince Regent than as the King. Behind his back people called him "Prinny." He had grown old and fat, waiting to ascend the throne. While he was Prince Regent he built a huge and odd-looking palace or pavilion for himself in the seaside town of Brighton. After his death, the ghost of this corpulent monarch was seen waddling down the long subterranean passage of the pavilion. Several other ghosts were also associated with the Brighton Pavilion. The curious structure was finally given to the city of Brighton which made it into a tourist attraction. Once the general public was allowed in, the royal ghost departed forever.

Actually George IV was more famous for seeing a ghost than being one. In 1786, while he was still the Prince Regent, he was a guest at Raynham Hall, a magnificent mansion in Norfolk. The hall also contains one of England's most celebrated ghosts, The Brown Lady. Just who this phantom is, or was, has been the subject of much controversy. But a lot of prominent people have reported seeing her. She has been described as a young woman wearing a brown dress. Her hair is disheveled, her face is pale, and some say that she has no eyes!

The Prince Regent, who was staying at Raynham Hall, awoke one evening to find a ghastly-looking woman in a brown dress standing beside his bed. The royal visitor fled the room in his nightshirt, screaming all the way. He roused everybody in the house, and when they were thoroughly awake he announced that he would not stay at Raynham Hall for another hour. True to his word, he got dressed and, followed by a crowd of his personal servants and hangers-on, he left, never to return.

The next king, William IV, was commonly known as "Silly Billy." His seven-year reign was so undistinguished that he does not even seem to have left a ghost behind.

Then there was Queen Victoria. She came to the throne in 1837, when she was only eighteen years old. She died in 1901, making her not only the longest reigning British monarch but the second-longest reigning monarch of any kind ever. In case you are interested, the record is held by Pepi II, a king of ancient Egypt who became pharaoh when he was about two years old, and died at the age of ninety-two.

Victoria gave her name to an age—the Victorian period, when the British Empire stretched around the world. It was a time of enormous progress in the areas of science and technology. And it was also a period during which people were absolutely fascinated by the subject of ghosts.

Spiritualism, the belief that communication with the dead is possible with the aid of a specially sensitive person called a medium, began and flourished during the Victorian age. Spiritualism started in America but soon spread to England, where it was enormously popular. It was also the period which saw the start of the British Society for Psychical Research, the first organization in the world which tried to study the subject of ghosts scientifically.

Was the queen herself interested in the subject? It is impossible to answer that question with absolute certainty. In Victoria's day the private life of the royal family was just that, private. No palace servants went out and wrote "tell-all" books. There were no tapes of embarrassing phone conversations leaked to the tabloid press. In fact, if something embarrassing about the queen or her family was known to the press it wouldn't be printed. It just "wasn't done"; indeed an editor could go to jail for such an offense. But it's hard to believe that the queen was not interested. Many of the people that she knew well were deeply interested in ghosts. There are many rumors of séances in Buckingham Palace or other royal residences. How could the queen possibly have avoided the general fascination?

We do know for certain that she was obsessed by death. She married a German prince named Albert, and was completely devoted to him. But Albert died in 1861 and the queen spent the remaining forty years of her life as a widow. She dressed only in black for many years, and for long periods refused to go out in public. The royal residences were littered with mournful memorials to the dead prince. She often indicated to members of the government that she was somehow in communication with "Dear Albert." Albert always seemed to be advising a pro-German policy. Once, she actually walked out of a council meeting, announcing that she wanted to consult with the dead Albert. When she returned, she said that she opposed any hostile action against Germany. This sort of thing drove members of her government nearly frantic. It was difficult enough for them to deal with a willful living queen—but a dead German prince—that was too much.

William Gladstone was the prime minister who served longest under Queen Victoria. He was extremely interested in the subject of life after death. He became a member of the Society for Psychical Research and called the activities of the group "the most important work that is being done in the world—by far the most important."

However, the queen never liked Gladstone, because he sometimes disagreed with her, and she couldn't stand that. On the other hand, she became devoted to one of her other prime ministers, the eccentric Benjamin Disraeli. Disraeli had a system for handling the queen: "I never deny; I never contradict; I sometimes forget."

Disraeli and the queen were involved in a famous

incident with supernatural overtones. They were traveling together on a nighttime railway journey to the queen's residence in Scotland when the train suddenly stopped. The queen asked Disraeli to find out what had happened. The prime minister went to the front of the train, and the engineer told him that he stopped because there was a ghostly figure dancing on the tracks ahead. Disraeli walked around the engine and found that a large moth, probably attracted by the light, had become attached to the headlamp. The shadow it cast looked like a dancing figure.

Because of the stop, the royal party's train was delayed for nearly half an hour. Within a few moments the train was forced to stop again, this time because there was a warning signal. A large tree had fallen across the track farther up the line and would have wrecked the royal train if it had not stopped. The delay caused by the moth had given the railway men time to locate the tree and light the warning signal.

Disraeli was in London during his last illness. He was asked if he would like the queen to be invited to come and see him. "No, better not," he replied wearily. "She'll only ask me to take a message to Albert. . . ."

The queen did visit Disraeli's country home of Hughenden Manor after the statesman's death. She said that she "sensed" his presence in his study. Others have reported actually seeing Disraeli's ghost. Hughenden has now become one of England's more celebrated haunted houses.

After Victoria died, her ghost was reportedly seen in many different places, but most frequently at Osborne House, the queen's favorite residence. But the strangest and most poignant appearance of Victoria's ghost is at Windsor Castle. This is the story:

The queen was not very fond of her eldest son Bertie (who became King Edward VII). He was lazy, lecherous, and not very bright. But most of all she blamed him for the death of her beloved Albert. While Bertie was in college at Cambridge, he got into trouble. Bertie was always getting into trouble, and in the autumn of 1861 Albert traveled down to Cambridge to try to sort things out for his erring son. The weather was very wet and Albert caught a bad cold. In December he died.

The queen always held Bertie responsible for his father's fatal illness. For months she couldn't stand the sight of him. In truth, she blamed him unfairly, for Albert died of typhoid fever, which had nothing to do with the cold he got traveling to Cambridge. But the queen would never accept that explanation.

Bertie married Princess Alexandra of Denmark in March 1863. There was a magnificent wedding ceremony held at Windsor Castle. The queen, however, was still in deep mourning over the death of Albert and had not forgiven her son for the part she believed he had played in it. She did not wish to attend the ceremony, but she could not entirely avoid the wedding of the future king either.

The queen was installed in a balcony, heavily curtained in black and purple velvet, high above the altar in the chapel. From time to time, servants would draw back the curtains so the queen could view the proceedings below. She was dressed all in black, save for a bright blue sash. As soon as she thought she saw someone looking at her, she would have the curtains closed. This strange procedure continued throughout the entire ceremony. In recent years, visitors to the chapel have looked up to see the figure of a rather stout lady, all dressed in black, seated alone in a high balcony. She appears to be looking down on the passing tourists.

Of course, the guards in the chapel assure all who ask that there is no person in the balcony. No living person, that is.

CHAPTER THREE

Lincoln's Restless Assassins

OF ALL THE GHOSTS that reportedly haunt the United States, that of the murdered President Abraham Lincoln is by far the best known. His ghost has been reported everywhere from the White House in Washington, to Springfield, Illinois, where he is buried, and all points in between.

But what of those who plotted and carried out the assassination? Do their spirits rest easy? Not according to the stories told around Washington, D.C., and Maryland. The entire Lincoln assassination appears to be enveloped in a ghostly fog.

The assassination of President Lincoln was planned and carried out by a group of Southern sympathizers headed by the actor John Wilkes Booth. The plotters met at a Washington boarding house on H Street between Sixth and Seventh. The boarding house was owned by Mary Surratt. Her son, John, was one of the conspirators. Whether Mary Surratt herself was actually part of the plot is something that historians have argued about for years. The evidence is not entirely clear. But in the near hysteria that gripped Washington after the assassination, there were no doubts.

At midnight on the night Lincoln was shot, April 14, 1865, police and federal troops rousted Mary Surratt out of bed, accused her of being a conspirator, and took her off to prison in a building called the Old Brick Capitol. She always protested her innocence, and said though Booth had visited the boarding house often enough, she barely knew him, and had no idea of what was being planned. It did no good. She was tried, convicted, and hanged with other conspirators on July 7, 1865.

Within a few years, strange stories began to circulate about the H Street boarding house. After Mary's execution it became the property of her daughter, Annie, who sold it at a much reduced price. It was not a popular piece of property and one new owner followed the other in such rapid succession that it soon began to attract the attention of journalists.

They began interviewing people who had once owned the place. They spoke of "mumblings" and "muffled sounds" as if a group of men were talking together in low voices. Some said that they could actually hear details of the assassination plot being discussed. Others reported that they could hear footsteps pacing up and back in the room which had once been Mary's bedroom. It was said that Mary's ghost was doomed to walk around Washington for all eternity, or until her name was cleared. Current owners, naturally, said they heard nothing. The place had a bad enough reputation. If it was also haunted, that would bring the selling price down further.

The old boarding house has been renovated many times. During the 1970s it was a Chinese grocery store. There have been no recent reports of ghostly occurrences there, though the owners may just be sticking to the old tradition of not talking about it.

Mary Surratt had originally come from Maryland about thirteen miles south of Washington, where she and her husband John had run a farm. When the area around their farm became more populated they turned part of their house into a general store and tavern. They were quite well-known in the area, and in fact the community was called Surrattville for many years. Immediately after the execution the name was changed to Clinton. The new name has nothing to do with President Bill Clinton or anyone in his family.

After the death of her husband, Mary Surratt and her two children had moved to Washington. They leased their old Maryland house to John Lloyd, a former Washington policeman turned tavern keeper.

The Surratt family remained on friendly terms with Lloyd, and visited his tavern regularly. The house may also have figured in the assassination plot. After shooting Lincoln, Booth headed for the old Surratt tavern in order to pick up supplies. He apparently never got there, and Lloyd himself was not suspected. Indeed, he gave evidence against Mary and her son at the trial.

The old tavern had a number of owners over the years, reputedly including Edwin Booth, the assassin's brother and a very famous actor. The old tavern's association with the Lincoln assassination was nearly forgotten. It would have been entirely forgotten were it not for reports of muffled voices and mumblings similar to those in the Surratt boarding house. An even more striking manifestation is the figure of a woman wearing a long black dress, that is seen on the old building's broad porch.

The figure is said to be that of Mary Surratt herself. Perhaps she is revisiting a place where she spent happier days, or perhaps she is looking for the man who turned her in.

Mary Surratt's ghost is an exceptionally active one. Directly after her arrest she was taken to the Old Brick Capitol. The building had served temporarily as the Capitol building, but during the Civil War it had been converted into a prison. For several years, on the anniversary of Mary Surratt's death, the outline of a female figure was seen against one of the windows. One witness reported that the figure sobbed incessantly while clenching her "ghostly white fists against black iron bars" that were also part of the apparition.

The Old Brick Capitol was also said to be haunted by a number of other ghosts, from Senator John C. Calhoun, who lived there when it was an apartment building to Confederate spy Belle Boyd, who was imprisoned there. But the structure no longer exists. It was torn down to make room for the new Supreme Court building.

Mary Surratt and three of the other conspirators were hanged on the grounds of the old Arsenal Penitentiary, not far from Capitol Hill. Their bodies were buried near the gallows but later moved to permanent graves. There is a tale that Mary's spirit somehow influenced the mysterious growth of a boxwood tree on the site that marked the scaffold. Legend has it that this is just one more way of her trying to attract attention and prove her innocence.

The death sentence on Mary Surratt and the other conspirators was pronounced by Judge Advocate General Joseph Holt. Though he had always been known as a taciturn and ill-mannered man with few friends, after the conspiracy trial he became a virtual recluse. He is said to have locked himself in his house and spent most of his time rereading the transcripts of the famous trial. After he died, the new owners of the house claimed that they heard his remorseful spirit pacing up and down in his room for hours on end.

When the house was torn down, Judge Holt's spirit, wearing a midnight-blue Union uniform, was reported walking down First Street. The legend says that he is on his way to the Old Brick Capitol to question Mary Surratt once again.

After Booth shot Lincoln at Ford's Theatre he jumped from the box in which the president had been sitting and onto the stage to make his escape. There is an enduring legend that any actor or actress who attempts to speak his or her lines along the route across the stage where Booth made his escape will become hopelessly muddled. Booth broke his leg during the jump, but still managed to join fellow conspirator David Herold, who was waiting with horses, and astonishingly they were able to elude their pursuers.

At four o'clock in the morning of April 15, 1865, Booth and Herold arrived at the house of Dr. Samuel Mudd in Charles County, Maryland. The doctor treated Booth's leg and housed both men until late in the afternoon.

Booth managed to avoid capture for twelve days, but he was finally found hiding in a barn near Bowling Green, Virginia. The barn was surrounded, set afire, and

Booth was shot. There is a controversy over whether he was shot trying to escape or if he killed himself. There are even rumors that he escaped to Mexico, where he lived under an assumed name. But this is highly improbable. Still, that may be why his ghost—unlike that of Mary Surratt—is rarely reported, though his footsteps have been heard around Ford's Theatre.

Dr. Mudd, like many of his Maryland neighbors, was a Southern sympathizer, and he had actually met John Wilkes Booth before the night of April 15. However, when he was arrested, he claimed that he had not recognized Booth, who was wearing a crude disguise, and had no idea what he had done.

While no solid proof of Dr. Mudd's connection to the conspiracy was ever presented, the circumstances certainly looked suspicious. He was tried and convicted by a military court and sentenced to life imprisonment at Fort Jefferson on Dry Tortugas Island, Florida. The conditions on the island prison were harsh and primitive. When a yellow-fever epidemic struck the island prison, Dr. Mudd was responsible for saving many lives. He was pardoned by President Andrew Johnson and returned to his home in 1869. But he lived under a cloud, and his health had been seriously affected by his prison experience. Dr. Mudd died in 1883.

Since his death, a small group made up primarily of the doctor's family members have energetically lobbied to clear his name, and they have had a modest degree of success. Nevertheless, unless some startling new evidence can be turned up, it is doubtful if many minds will be changed.

One of Mudd's grandchildren, Louise Mudd Arehart, has not only worked to clear the family name but has spent a lot of time restoring and preserving the Mudd farmhouse as an historically significant landmark. She was the last member of the Mudd family to be born in the old house. Furthermore, she says that her long-dead grandfather has encouraged her in this effort.

The ghost did not appear to her at the old family home, which had been abandoned and was falling apart. It showed up in her own house in La Plata, Maryland. At first there were the usual knockings and unexplained footsteps; there were the doors that opened and closed mysteriously. But soon the ghostly figure itself made an appearance. It was a man dressed in black trousers and a vest. He wore a white shirt with sleeves rolled up to the elbows. The figure was first seen outside the house, and then right inside the house. Once Mrs. Arehart almost ran into him as she was going through the doorway in the dining room. The house was thoroughly searched but no trace of the mysterious intruder could be found.

Though she never saw the face of the ghostly figure clearly, Mrs. Arehart became convinced that what she was seeing was the ghost of her grandfather Dr. Samuel Mudd. Why had he decided to appear after all these years? She thought she knew. He had come back to find someone who would help to preserve the old family home. Mrs. Arehart took on the task with a great deal of energy and not only raised the money to have the house partially restored but also arranged to have it listed on the National Register of Historic Places. It's now open to the public, but the ghost of Dr. Mudd, apparently feeling his task was complete, has not been seen there.

Just to complete the roll of ghosts associated with the Lincoln assassination, there is the tragic Major Henry Rathbone. Major Rathbone was seated with President Lincoln when he went to Ford's Theatre on that fatal night. He was stabbed in the neck by Booth before the assassin jumped to the stage.

The major was critically injured but he recovered from his wounds—his physical wounds, that is. His mind never seemed to recover. Before the assassination he had been a brilliant and successful army officer, married to the daughter of a New York senator. Afterward he became moody and distracted. He resigned from the army and moved with his wife and family to Germany. The change of scene did nothing for him. One night, shortly before Christmas, he shot his wife and would have killed his children as well if their quick-thinking nurse had not saved them. Rathbone turned the gun on himself. He survived, but spent the rest of his days in an insane asylum.

Though the tragic events had taken place an ocean away from Washington, news soon spread among friends and former neighbors of the Rathbone family. As people walked along Jackson Street, they would often cross the street over to the park, rather than walk directly in front of what had been the Rathbone house. There was a general feeling that the house had somehow been caught up in the web of tragedy which seemed to have trapped so many who had been associated with the Lincoln assassination. Rumors spread that the cries and sobs of a man could be heard coming from the old house. For a time the house on Jackson Street had the reputation of being one of the most haunted places in Washington, a city which already had more than its fair share of hauntings.

CHAPTER FOUR

The Past Lives
of General Patton

GENERAL GEORGE S. PATTON was one of the genuine
heroes of World War II. He was a brilliant, if
somewhat eccentric, tank commander. His life was the
basis for the film *Patton*, which deservedly won a whole
flock of Academy Awards in 1970. Actor George C.
Scott's Oscar-winning portrayal of the general is regarded as one of the great performances in movie history.

Patton came from a military family and graduated
from West Point in 1909. During World War I he served
in the newly formed tank corps, and between the wars

he was one of the most vocal supporters of the use of tank power in future wars.

During World War II he got a chance to prove his theories. He led the tank corps in North Africa, and commanded the Seventh Army in its drive across Sicily. But his great accomplishment was in leading the Third Army in its triumphant sweep across France in the summer of 1944.

Patton had his own ideas about how wars should be fought, and he didn't hesitate to ignore or flat-out disobey orders when they conflicted with his very strong opinions about what should be done. His superior officers acknowledged his brilliance as a field commander, but he also drove them nearly frantic with his absolute certainty that he, and only he, knew the right way to fight a battle.

Patton was a soldier's officer, not a man to be tied down at a desk many miles behind the front lines. He shared the hardships and dangers of his men; in fact, his troops called him "Old Blood and Guts." But he was a hard-driving disciplinarian and he wasn't always popular with his men. In one well-publicized incident the general publicly slapped a soldier he believed had shown cowardice. In truth, Patton was wrong and it nearly cost him his command.

General Patton was killed in an automobile accident in Germany in 1945. His body was to be shipped back to the United States for burial, but when his wife heard that not all of the American soldiers killed in Europe would be returned, she said that he would want to be buried with his men. "I know that George would want to lie beside the men of his army who have fallen," she said. And so he did, in the American cemetery in Luxembourg, the cemetery with the largest number of Third Army casualties.

There can be no doubt that General Patton was a soldier. But he was sure that he had been more than a soldier in the twentieth century: He was convinced that he had been a soldier throughout human history. The general believed in reincarnation. That is the doctrine which holds that people are "reborn" in different bodies at different times. Reincarnation is basic to many Eastern religions, but it is not part of Western tradition.

Just how General Patton came to this belief is unknown, but his nephew Fred Ayer, who wrote a biography of the general, once asked him:

"Uncle George, do you really believe in reincarnation?"

The general answered, "I don't know about other people; but for myself there has never been any question. I don't just think it, I know there are places I've been before, and not in this life."

General Patton also believed that he would be reborn as a soldier to fight in future wars. He even wrote a poem about his beliefs. It ends with these words:

So forever in the future,
Shall I battle as of yore
Dying to be born a fighter
But to die again once more.

The most striking example of his belief in reincarnation occurred during World War I when Patton was a young man. He had been posted to Langres, a small town in northeastern France, where he was to operate a tank school. He had never been in the area before, and a French liaison officer offered to show him around. "You don't have to," said Patton. "I know this place, I know it well."

The area had once been the site of a Roman military camp. Patton was sure that he had been there before as a Roman soldier. As he was driven through the area the American soldier was able to direct his French driver to the old Roman drill ground, to the Roman forum, and to the temples of Mars and Apollo, even though these structures had disappeared long ago, and the locations were known only to archaeologists. He even pointed out the site where Julius Caesar had made his camp when he visited the area over two thousand years ago. "It was," he told his nephew, "as if someone were at my ear whispering the directions."

Aside from his belief that he had fought with Caesar, he believed he had been a soldier in ancient Greece, that he was in the army that had opposed the Huns' invasion of Europe, that he had been a Crusader, and that he rode with the Highland Scots in defense of the House of Stuart in England.

When he was in North Africa during World War II, a British officer complimented him on his boldness. "You'd have made a great marshal for Napoleon if you had lived during the eighteenth century." Patton merely grinned. "But I did," he said.

CHAPTER FIVE

The Many Hauntings of Edgar Allan Poe

LET US GET something straight from the very beginning. Edgar Allan Poe never wrote any ghost stories. Most people seem to think that he did, but he didn't.

Poe was one of the most famous and influential writers America ever produced. No other American writer of his era, which was the first half of the nineteenth century, is as well-known and widely read today. He developed the art of the short story more than any writer who had gone before him. He practically invented the detective story. He was a pioneer of what we would now call science fiction. He even wrote a lot of humor, though to tell the truth, his humorous stories are not very good, because Poe was not naturally a funny man.

The Poe book that sold best during his lifetime was a popular science work on mollusks or shellfish. Poe was proudest of his poetry, and always thought that he would be best remembered as a poet. But aside from *The Raven* and a couple of other gloomy works, no one reads Poe's poetry today.

What Edgar Allan Poe's fame rests on are his tales of terror, not supernatural terror, but real or psychological terror. In *The Pit and the Pendulum,* for example, the terror, the prospect of being sliced up by a swinging blade, is quite real. In *The Fall of the House of Usher,* Roderick Usher is not afraid of the ghost of his sister, Madeline, it is Madeline herself he fears. He thinks she has been buried alive, a common fear in Poe's day, and one that recurs in several of his tales.

In stories like *The Tell-Tale Heart* or *Ligeia,* the ghostly events are really a product of the narrator's fevered imagination. It is quite clear that the narrator is losing or has already lost his mind. These are tales of psychological terror. *The Masque of the Red Death* is allegory.

The closest Poe ever gets to a "real" ghost story is *The Facts in the Case of M Valdemar.* In this story a man named Valdemar is mesmerized or hypnotized just at the point of death, and is therefore kept in a half-alive state, though he is actually dead. The story is really science fiction, but when it was first published in 1845 Poe was astonished to discover that a lot of people thought it was true. In Poe's day hypnotism had an almost magical reputation.

Did Poe himself believe in ghosts? I don't really know, but somehow I doubt it. He never showed any particular interest in spiritualism, which became extremely popular during his lifetime. He certainly never wrote about it, though lots of other writers did.

So, as I said, Edgar Allan Poe never wrote any real ghost stories. But you will never convince most people of that. I know I have been trying for years. Nobody listens.

Another reason that most people connect Poe with ghost stories is that the writer himself led such a strange and tragic life. He died when he was relatively young, and under very mysterious circumstances. Almost immediately after his death all sorts of legends began to be spun around him, and soon it became impossible to separate fact from myth. Ghost stories have been written *about* Poe. And, as you might expect, many people have reported seeing his ghost in various places associated with his life.

Poe was born in Boston in 1809 but was raised in Richmond, Virginia, and received much of his early education in England and Scotland. He briefly attended West Point, which he hated, and spent most of his adult life moving from place to place along the East Coast. He was forever in search of a literary job with decent pay. He never found one. He was usually in debt and managed to quarrel violently with practically everyone who would have been able to help him. He spent a lot of time in New York and Philadelphia. But the city with which Poe is most associated is Baltimore. He lived there for years. That's where he died and where his ghost has been seen most frequently.

Throughout his life Poe's enemies, and he had loads of them, said he was a drunk. This may not be fair, for he does not seem to have been a particularly heavy drinker for early-nineteenth-century America, where heavy drinking was common. He was always an extremely hard worker, and never missed a day of work because he was drunk. But Poe did have a problem with alcohol. Even a small amount seemed to have an enormous effect upon him.

In 1847, after the death of his wife, Poe became seriously ill. He was taken to see a famous doctor who diagnosed him as having a "brain lesion," some sort of brain injury. The doctor also said Poe did not have long to live. Medical knowledge of the brain was pretty sketchy in 1847, and there is still debate over what might have really been wrong with him. But whatever it was, it may have accounted for his inability to tolerate alcohol, and his often erratic behavior.

In late September 1849, Poe, who had been living in Richmond, traveled up to Baltimore. According to one account, he attended a birthday party, took one glass of wine for a toast, left the party and disappeared. The next five days are a complete blank. On October third he was found wandering the streets mumbling incoherently. He was taken to the Church Home Hospital in Baltimore, where he died without ever regaining his senses so he could tell people where he had been.

No one knows what happened to Poe during those final, and fatal, five days. One popular story is that the drunken or drugged Poe was taken by a group of crooked politicians from polling place to polling place, so that he could vote many times. There is no particular reason to believe that the story is true.

Poe was buried behind the Westminster Presbyterian Church in Baltimore. There is a marker which commemorates the spot. Later his remains were moved to the Poe family plot in the same churchyard.

The figure of a man, dressed in black early-nineteenth-century clothes, has been seen staggering through the streets of the old section of Baltimore, much as Poe might have done during those five days when he disappeared. The same figure has also been reported in the corridors of the hospital where he died.

Many visitors have reported the spectral figure of Edgar Allan Poe in the Westminster Presbyterian churchyard, both near the spot of his original burial and his final resting place.

But the most striking ghostly events are connected with what is called the Poe House in Baltimore. Poe lived in a lot of different houses during his life. Most of them were torn down long ago. But from 1832 to 1835 Poe lived in a very plain, two-and-a-half-story house at 203 North Amity Street, Baltimore. Poe had just been kicked out of West Point and was broke, as usual. When he came to the house, three of his relatives were already living there—his grandmother Elizabeth Poe, his Aunt Maria Clemm, and his young cousin Virginia Clemm. Later Poe married Virginia, but it was Mrs. Clemm who really kept the family together, and supported Poe when no one else would. Mrs. Clemm and Virginia are now buried beside him.

A lot of different people lived in the little house until 1922, when it became vacant and probably would have been torn down if it had not been rescued by the Edgar Allan Poe Society and restored as an historical monument and museum to commemorate the writer.

During the 1960s a large number of visitors to the little house reported being tapped on the shoulder by an unseen hand. But the most dramatic manifestation came in 1968. There were riots in Baltimore, and the police were called because someone had spotted mysterious lights inside the Poe House. They were afraid that intruders had gotten in and might set fire to the place.

When the police arrived they found the door was locked, but they could see the light which moved from the first to the second floor and then to the garret, where Poe himself had lived. They didn't want to break down the door of an historic house, so they surrounded the place and waited for a tour guide to arrive the next morning and let them in. The house was empty. No one could have gotten in, or out, and the source of the light remains a complete mystery. The story got a lot of publicity. More than any other incident this one established the reputation of the Poe House as being haunted.

There were other strange events in the house. In 1980 a radio station sponsored a Halloween séance in the Poe House. Before the séance, voices were heard coming from the garret, but when people went upstairs to investigate they found no one. In 1984 an acting troupe was putting on a dramatic presentation of one of Poe's stories in the house. Shortly before the performance, a window in what had been Virginia's room had been mysteriously pulled out of the frame and smashed on the floor. The actress who had been using the room as her dressing room was terrified.

And of course, there are the usual doors that open and close by themselves and the mysterious footsteps typical of a haunted house.

The Poe House reputation for being haunted is so strong that the street gangs which abound in this poor and run-down neighborhood just stay away from the place.

There is one more rather macabre story attached to Poe's death. It seems that each year on January 19, the anniversary of his death, someone places roses and a bottle of brandy on the Poe grave. It's a gesture the writer might have appreciated.

Not long ago Jeff Jerome, who is the curator of the

Poe House in Baltimore, decided to try to find out who the mysterious visitor may be. He and four other Poe fans staked out the grave. After waiting for several hours, they heard the cemetery gates rattle at about 1:30 A.M. When they turned on a flashlight the intruder fled, but not before Jerome and his friend Ann Byerly caught a glimpse of him.

Byerly describes the mysterious stranger as a man with blond or brown hair, who was wearing a dramatic-looking frock coat. "He was clutching a walking stick with a golden sphere on its end—like the one Poe carried." Jerome added, "Before vanishing over the wall, he raised his cane high in the air and shook it at us triumphantly."

Maybe Edgar Allan Poe himself never wrote a ghost story and maybe he didn't believe in ghosts, but an awful lot of people today believe in Poe's ghost and have been telling stories about it. He also seems to have some pretty strange fans as well.

CHAPTER SIX

Mark Twain's Dream of Death

SAMUEL CLEMENS, better known as Mark Twain, is one of America's most celebrated writers. His books include the classics *Tom Sawyer* and *Huckleberry Finn*. He was about as tough-minded and skeptical an individual as anyone could possibly be. Yet, when he was young he had a strange and terrifying experience that haunted him for the rest of his life.

Before he became a writer, Sam Clemens was a pilot on the riverboats that steamed up and down the mighty Mississippi. It was a job that he loved, and he wrote about his experiences in *Life on the Mississippi*.

In 1858 Sam was serving as a cub pilot on the steamboat *Pennsylvania* which ran between St. Louis and

New Orleans. He was able to find a job for his younger brother Henry on the boat. It wasn't a glamorous job like being a riverboat pilot. Henry's position was pretty lowly, as its title "mud clerk" would indicate. Still, though the hours were long and the pay was poor, there was the promise of promotion. Besides, jobs were hard to come by and Henry seemed content.

While in St. Louis, Sam stayed with his sister and brother-in-law, the Moffetts. Pilots had no duties while the steamer was in port. Mud clerks did, and Henry, who worked long hours and slept on the boat, usually visited the Moffett house only in the evening.

One night shortly before the *Pennsylvania* was due to return to New Orleans, Henry visited as usual. But he seemed unusually solemn. When he left to go back to the ship, he shook hands all around. His mother, who was also staying at the house, felt something was wrong though she wasn't sure what it might be.

That night Sam Clemens had a horrifying dream. He saw his brother's corpse laid out in a metal coffin that had been set between two chairs in the Moffetts' sitting room. He wore one of Sam's suits. There was an arrangement of flowers, roses, on his chest. All the flowers were white, except for one bright red rose in the center.

Perhaps you have had the experience of waking up from a dream that is so vivid for a while you are convinced it was real. That is how Sam Clemens felt. He could not go into the room where he was sure his brother's coffin lay. He dressed quickly and took a walk. Once out in the air, he realized that Henry could not be dead. He rushed back to the house and into the sitting room. It was empty, there was no casket. It had all been a dream! Yet the dream had seemed so profoundly real that he could not shake the image from his mind.

He boarded the *Pennsylvania* and on the trip downriver, Sam, who had a quick temper, fought with the master of the ship and was fired. That probably saved his life.

Sam Clemens was stuck in New Orleans, but he got a temporary job as a night watchman. The *Pennsylvania,* with Henry on board, left New Orleans for the trip back to St. Louis.

We may think of a trip on a riverboat steamer as a romantic and certainly safe experience. The ships, however, were anything but safe. Accidents, particularly explosions of the steam boilers, were common. And that is what happened to the *Pennsylvania* a few miles below Memphis. Debris was scattered for hundreds of yards, killing passengers and crew. In addition to the dead, three dozen people were severely injured. One of them was Henry Clemens.

Sam had gotten a job aboard another steamer which was running about one day behind the *Pennsylvania.* News of the explosion had spread downriver, and Sam heard details of the story at towns along the river. When he got to Memphis he found his brother in a large warehouse which had hurriedly been converted into a hospital for those injured in the *Pennsylvania* disaster.

Henry was among the most seriously injured. He had inhaled steam, and the doctors held out little hope that he would survive. Sam convinced one of the doctors to pay special attention to Henry, who had almost been given up as a hopeless case. Much to everyone's surprise, Henry seemed to respond to the treatment. A week after Sam Clemens had found his critically injured brother near death, there was now a good chance that he was going to recover.

But still the young man was in great pain. The medical practice of the time was to administer morphine as a painkiller. But someone accidentally gave Henry Clemens too much of the powerful drug, and he died, not from his injuries, but from an overdose of morphine.

Sam was not at the hospital when his brother died. By the time he arrived, the corpse had been taken to what was called the "dead room" and laid out in a metal coffin. Henry was dressed in one of Sam's suits for all of his own clothes had been destroyed in the explosion. As Sam Clemens watched, an old woman came in and put a bouquet of flowers on his brother's chest. The bouquet was made up of white roses with a single red rose in the center.

Suddenly the image from the dream came back to Samuel Clemens with painful clarity. All that was lacking was the coffin being set between two chairs in the Moffett sitting room.

Sam rode with his brother's coffin back to St. Louis. As soon as the boat docked he rushed to his brother-in-law's office. But they crossed paths. Moffett was already on his way to the boat to claim the body and have it sent to his home.

Sam now hurried to the Moffett house. He wanted to get there before the coffin arrived. He did not want the coffin opened so that his mother could see Henry's ravaged body. He arrived before the coffin, and went upstairs to the sitting room. There he found two chairs set six feet apart. The coffin was to be placed on them. That would have fulfilled the final detail of his dream of death.

CHAPTER SEVEN

The Great Lover's Ghost

FROM TIME TO TIME scenes from Rudolph Valentino's old films like *The Sheik* or *The Four Horsemen of the Apocalypse* are shown on television. The great lover crosses his arms, rolls his eyes and flares his nostrils. That is supposed to be oh-so-romantic, but it looks oh-so-silly.

Yet it is wrong to judge the idols of one age by the standards of another. Back in the 1920s Valentino was Bogart, Redford and Luke Perry all rolled into one and doubled. There is no movie star today who has the sort of fanatical following that Valentino inspired. He was the first really great romantic figure of the silent movies.

The journalist H. L. Mencken said he was "catnip to women." Men didn't like him very much.

Valentino rocketed to stardom in 1921. He made a relative handful of films. He married twice, and was the constant subject of gossip and scandal. More than once his brief career seemed at the point of collapse.

To tell the truth he was not a very good actor; in fact, he was not much of an actor at all, he was more of a screen personality. He might not even be remembered today except that in 1926 Rudolph Valentino, age thirty-one, did something which ensured his fame. He died suddenly under circumstances which seemed to some mysterious. He was still young and good-looking. His fans never saw him grow old. In their eyes he would eternally be the great lover. It is the reaction to Valentino's death, rather than his life, which is most striking.

On August 14, 1926, Valentino was in a New York hotel when he suddenly fell to the floor, grasping his stomach in pain. His illness made headline news throughout the world. Every medical bulletin was eagerly awaited by his fans. The streets around the hospital in which he lay were lined with fans day and night. Valentino's condition steadily worsened, and on August 23 he was dead. According to the doctors, the great lover died as a result of complications from a perforated ulcer and a ruptured appendix. Many of his fans did not believe the diagnosis and there were rumors that he had been poisoned, that the perforations in his stomach had been caused by ground glass that had been put in his food, or that he had actually been shot in the stomach. No one seemed to be able to agree as to who the murderer was, and what the motive may have been. Speculation, however, was endless. It makes the more recent speculation over Marilyn Monroe's death look tame and restrained by comparison.

The actor's death set off a frenzy quite unlike anything that had ever been seen in America before or since. Several women committed suicide, clutching Valentino photographs. When the screen idol's body was put on display in a Manhattan funeral chapel it was besieged by tens of thousands of weeping women. All traffic in the area was blocked. The coffin was partially closed so that only Valentino's head could be seen. The funeral director feared that fans might try to grab pieces of clothing or jewelry as souvenirs.

The next day, the crowds were even larger and more unruly. The funeral parlor's large plate-glass window was broken by the crush of the crowd and three women were injured. Alarmed and disgusted by the excesses of the fans, Valentino's manager cut short the planned week of public viewing for the body. Valentino's casket was sent west in a locked railroad car. But word of the journey leaked out, and in Chicago a mob of women tried to break into the car. They did not succeed but there were many injuries. In Los Angeles authorities took the precaution of secretly unloading the casket at an isolated suburban station to avoid the hysterical throngs that had gathered at the main depot.

After a frenzied funeral, Valentino's body was laid to rest in Hollywood Memorial Park Cemetery in Los Angeles. In the 1930s a mysterious "woman in black" began appearing at his crypt for the yearly commemorative services marking his death. The eerie, heavily veiled figure would lay a single rose on the tomb and disappear without speaking to anyone. Soon others began to imitate the original, and at one time there were as many as a dozen "women in black" who showed up at the service. The identity of many of these veiled figures remains unknown. One of them turned out to be Ditra Flame, president of the Hollywood Valentino Memorial Guild, dedicated to keeping the memory of the great lover fresh. She continued to appear every year until the 1960s.

There are still Valentino fan clubs today. There have also been a number of biographies and several not very successful attempts to make films about his life. Those projects have gone so badly wrong so many times that they are considered jinxed.

Aside from the rumors of murder there were also rumors that Valentino had somehow been "cursed." One of the tales was told by a man named Chaw Mank, a dancer turned celebrity psychic consultant, who had known Valentino at the height of his career. Mank ran into Valentino in Chicago in 1923, where the star was on an exhibition dance tour while waiting out a contract dispute with his studio.

Mank noticed that Valentino was wearing a large ring with a striking "cat's-eye" stone. Rudy, as his friends called him, was very fond of gaudy ornaments, but this one stood out. Mank commented on it and the star said that he bought it in San Francisco's Chinatown, and was told it was a "destiny ring." The shopkeeper who sold it to him said that it would bring him good luck.

"What do you see as my destiny?" he asked Mank.

Mank agreed Valentino's luck would take a turn for the better. "I see your career taking an upswing very soon. I see you settling your differences with the studio and working out a better deal with another studio. . . ."

He hesitated, for he also foresaw an untimely and painful death. As he started to continue his prediction, Valentino raised a hand. "You see it will bring good luck, just as the shopkeeper said." Like so many others, the great silent screen idol didn't want to hear any bad news.

Valentino did settle his contract dispute and then went on to sign an even better contract with another studio, and his career, which had been flagging, took off once again. He also died an unexpected and painful death—which many considered mysterious.

The next time Mank saw the cat's-eye ring it was on the finger of a popular singer named Russ Columbo.

Columbo had been signed to play Valentino in a screen biography.

Mank tried to warn him off the ring, but Columbo thought it was all nonsense. The singer was killed in an auto accident shortly before filming was to begin on the Valentino story.

The ring was inherited by Joe Casino, a close friend of Columbo's. He knew about its history and swore he would never wear it until the curse had time to "wear off." For several years he kept the ring in a display case, but then he figured enough time had passed, and he put it on. A few days later, he was hit by a truck and killed.

Today, the whereabouts of the ring are unknown.

During his career, Rudolph Valentino made a lot of money, and spent even more. When he died he was deeply in debt, despite his enormous popularity. One of the things he spent his money on was his Hollywood dream mansion, which he called Falcon Lair. The name came from *The Hooded Falcon*, a film Valentino very much wanted to make, but never did. Shortly after his death, eerie stories began circulating about Valentino's ghost haunting Falcon Lair.

There was a report that the mansion's caretaker was seen running down the canyon near the estate in the middle of the night screaming that he had just seen Valentino's ghost.

Another frequently repeated story was that one of the stablemen who had worked on the estate left so abruptly that he didn't even bother to collect his personal belongings. When friends asked him what happened he refused to talk. Months later he confided that he had come into the stable one evening and seen the spirit of the dead movie star petting his favorite horse.

A woman from Seattle who was staying in the house said that she heard mysterious footsteps and saw doors opening and closing. She never saw any ghost, but apparently Valentino's two watchdogs, Rudy and Brownie, did. These two dogs had been carefully trained to bark and snap at any intruders. But they merely whimpered and wagged their tails happily, as if they were in the presence of someone they knew very well but hadn't seen for a long time.

A jeweler who had contracted to buy Falcon Lair abruptly backed out of the deal. Rumors spread that Valentino's ghost didn't like the fellow and scared him away.

After his death, all sorts of people claimed that they were in contact with Valentino's spirit. His second wife, Natasha Rambova, who had managed (and some say mismanaged) much of his career, received a message from beyond the grave, saying that Valentino was in the next world where he longed to become "a legitimate actor."

CHAPTER EIGHT

Ghostly Encounters of the Stars

THE ACTOR TELLY SAVALAS is best known for the title role in the TV cop series "Kojak." One night he had an experience far stranger than anything that had ever been seen on his show.

The actor was driving home from a friend's house on Long Island, New York, very late one night. His car ran out of gas on a side road. Fortunately for Savalas, he was near an all-night diner. He asked the whereabouts of the nearest open gas station. He was told that he would have to take the path that ran through the woods at the back of the diner, and then walk until he reached the main highway where there was a gas station. It was a long walk, particularly in the dark, but Savalas had no choice.

As the actor told the story: "I was just about to set out when I heard someone ask in a high-pitched voice if I wanted a lift. I turned and saw a guy in a black Cadillac. I thanked him, climbed into the passenger seat, and we drove to the freeway.

"To my embarrassment, I had no wallet—it must have fallen out of my pocket. But the man loaned me a dollar. I insisted I must pay him back and got him to write his name and address on a scrap of paper. His name was Harry Agannis."

The next day Savalas tried to locate his benefactor. He found the name listed in the phone book and called. A woman answered the phone, and when the actor asked for Harry Agannis, he was met with a moment of silence. Then the woman explained that Harry Agannis had died three years earlier, and she was his widow.

After the initial shock wore off, Savalas concluded that he must have been the subject of a bizarre practical joke. But still he could not get the incident out of his mind. Finally he visited the house, and showed the woman the piece of paper which the man in the Cadillac had given him.

Savalas recalls, "When I showed her the paper she was obviously deeply affected and told me that without doubt it was her husband's handwriting. I described the clothes the man had worn. She said those were the same clothes Harry Agannis had been buried in."

The actor was completely puzzled. He had no idea why the ghost, if that's what it was, had chosen to befriend him.

"That was a case Kojak could not solve. I doubt if I'll ever be able to explain it."

Elke Sommer is a very glamorous German-born actress who became quite popular in American films during the 1960s. She and her husband, the Hollywood writer Joe Hyams, bought a house in Beverly Hills in July 1964 and soon discovered that the place was haunted. Their experiences in the house have been recounted in a number of magazine articles and in a book written by Hyams.

When they first moved into the place they were told that it was haunted by a spirit who wore a black jacket. They didn't believe the story. Then things began to happen. There were the usual ghostly footsteps, and doors that opened and closed mysteriously. Chairs seemed to be moved around, and other objects disappeared only to reappear a few days later in a different part of the house. There were even some sightings of a vague and ghostly figure wearing a black jacket.

Since Sommer and Hyams loved the house they decided they could put up with the inconvenience. The ghost was a nuisance, not a danger.

On March 13, 1967, the actress was awakened by noises coming from downstairs. She woke her husband and was trying to describe the sounds to him, when suddenly there was a loud and persistent pounding on the bedroom door.

Hyams jumped out of bed and ran to the door. When he pulled it open he was nearly overcome by a cloud of thick black smoke that billowed into the room. The dining room downstairs was on fire. The phone was still working, so they were able to call the fire department, but the smoke was so thick that they couldn't get through the hall to reach the front door.

Then they heard the pounding behind them, near a window. They looked out and realized that they could climb through it to the garage roof, and then easily drop to the ground.

The story was big news in Hollywood, where Sommer and Hyams were very well-known. Their house was invaded by a lot of people who called themselves psychics. Some were as annoying as the ghost itself. One theorized that the ghost had set the fire as an act of mischief and when it got out of hand, helped the couple escape.

Ultimately the couple decided this was one headache they did not need, and they sold the house. If the new owners were troubled by ghosts, they didn't say anything about it publicly.

♦ ♦ ♦

The folksinger-turned-actor Burl Ives had a strange story to tell Broadway columnist Danton Walker. It was about a visit he had made to Ireland.

"While driving to a house about an hour's ride from Dublin, I was sitting in the backseat of a small car. A woman friend was driving and another woman occupied the front seat alongside of her. We were heading for the home of a mutual friend to have dinner.

"About twenty minutes before we reached the house of our hostess, I noticed a figure standing in the road, directly in our path. It was getting dark, but even in that dim light I could tell that the figure was that of a man wearing a large cloak.

"Like most backseat drivers, I was tempted to cry out and warn the driver, but just before we reached the spot where the man had been standing, he disappeared. My impression was that he had paused only momentarily in the middle of the road, then had crossed over it, to the side that was bordered by a low stone wall. Beyond this wall was a sheer drop, which would have made an exit by this route very dangerous, unless a person were extremely surefooted. At the time, it occurred to me that whoever the person was, he was taking quite a chance to climb down that bank."

When Ives mentioned this to the two women in the front seat he was astonished to discover that neither of them had seen the figure, though he could not imagine how they could have missed it.

Later Ives described the incident to his hostess at dinner. She was not surprised. She said that a lot of people had seen the cloaked figure in the road—but then a lot of other people had not seen it.

According to local legends, she said, many years ago a holy man had sought refuge from the world in a nearby cave. But a woman found her way to the cave, and the temptation was too great for the holy man. Afterward, so the story went, the man was so overcome with remorse and guilt that he went half mad. He killed the woman, and then killed himself by jumping over the stone wall that borders the road, at the exact spot where Burl Ives had seen the cloaked figure disappear.

The actress and singer Gloria DeHaven, who was popular in films during the 1940s, credits a vision of her mother's ghost with saving her life.

She was driving one night when a terrible storm broke. She could barely see the road in front of her, and she considered stopping and waiting for the storm to blow over. But people were waiting for her, and besides she was on a deserted road and there was really no convenient place to pull off. To stop, she felt, would be more dangerous than to try to push on.

Then suddenly she saw what appeared to be a face on the windshield of her car. It looked like the face of her mother, who had been dead for many years. Then she saw that the vision had raised its right hand in what must have been a gesture of warning. At this point the actress decided that she had better stop.

Though the rain was coming down in buckets, she got out of her car to check the road ahead. She found that just a few yards ahead the road had been completely washed out. If she had hit that spot she might have been killed.

CHAPTER NINE

Clifton Webb
Wouldn't Leave

IT SEEMED AS IF Clifton Webb had been around forever. He was born in 1891 and began appearing on the stage as a child in 1902. He was an opera singer for a while and then became a popular nightclub song and dance man. His most successful dancing partner was Bonnie Glass, and when Webb moved on to Broadway musical comedies Glass found a new partner, a handsome young man named Rudolph Valentino.

On Broadway Webb was a leading man in a score of musicals. By the 1920s he was in Hollywood, appearing in a variety of musical and non-musical roles. Because of a contract dispute he turned down a musical role that was then offered to a virtual unknown named Fred Astaire. Astaire went on to become a huge star. Webb's career, however, floundered. While he was never out of work for long, the major stardom that was achieved by Valentino and Astaire always eluded him.

Then in 1944 Webb got the part of Waldo Lydecker in the mystery film *Laura*. The film has become a classic and Webb's performance as the conceited and overbearing columnist is really the best thing about it. In 1948 Webb did a light comedy called *Sitting Pretty*. He played Mr. Belvedere, an insufferably conceited literary man hired as a baby-sitter. It was a part similar to that of Waldo Lydecker. The character was not all that different from Clifton Webb himself. There was always something of the aristocratic English snob about Webb, although he was actually born in Indianapolis. *Sitting Pretty* was an enormous and unexpected success. There were two sequels and many years later, after Webb's death, it was the basis for the "Mr. Belvedere" television series.

When he was well into middle age, Clifton Webb achieved the kind of stardom that had been predicted for him since he had been a child. With his professional and financial future now secure Webb began looking around for a house that would fit his new status. He settled on a large Spanish-style, white stucco house in Beverly Hills. It was an area that was already home to many movie stars. The house Webb bought had previously been owned by other film people.

Webb lived in the house for twenty years. For most of that time he was extremely happy, though during his final few years he had become something of a recluse. He remodeled it a bit, to fit his own tastes, and added a room that he called his Greek room. Clifton Webb died in 1966.

In January of the following year the house was sold to a movie producer and his wife. The strange occurrences began almost immediately after the couple moved in. Small objects were moved around mysteriously, but the movement was not random or violent. For example, if a toothbrush was left on the sink it would later be found in the toothbrush holder. It was almost as if something were tidying up.

The new owners of the house turned the Greek room into a guest room, and that is where most of the strange happenings seemed to center. A guest staying in the room that Webb had designed found her cigarettes had been broken in half and tobacco scattered all over the bed. Clifton Webb had been a non-smoker who never hesitated to voice his anti-tobacco opinions.

The new owners had several dogs and cats and the animals seemed to sense that there was something wrong. They would not go near the Greek room; indeed, one of the dogs would sit at the door of the room howling loudly. Servants in the house found themselves pursued by an indefinable "presence," and the producer's secretary, who was working in the house at the time, found her files had been mysteriously rearranged.

The worst came one night in October. The dogs and cats had been exceptionally restless all day. Then in the middle of the night the producer and his wife were awakened by the sound of moaning in the bedroom. As they looked up they saw a grey smoky figure in the corner of the room.

The following morning they realized that it was the first anniversary of Clifton Webb's death.

The producer and his wife felt that there was something in the house that wasn't happy to have them there. Perhaps Webb didn't approve of the changes they had made in the house that he had lived in for so long and he was letting them know of his disapproval. So in January of 1968, when they were offered a great deal of money to sell the house, they seriously considered the offer. But after some discussion they decided that they liked the place so much that they would keep it, ghost and all. The very night they made the decision to keep the house they heard a mysterious voice in the bedroom saying, "Well, well," over and over again. The same phrase, "Well, well," was heard frequently for the next few days.

This incident was discussed with someone who had been a close friend of Clifton Webb during his lifetime. The friend reported that saying "Well, well, well, well" over and over again was a habit of the actor. He would often use the phrase for no apparent reason.

After that the ghost seemed to adopt a somewhat friendlier attitude toward the new residents. Perhaps he decided that they really did like and properly appreciate "his" house.

Ultimately the producer and his wife sold the house, and it has had several new owners since. There are reports that Clifton Webb is still hanging around. Perhaps after spending virtually his entire life on the stage or in the movies, he just can't give up the spotlight.

CHAPTER TEN

Superman's Ghost

THE YOUNG COUPLE was able to purchase the big house at 1579 Benedict Canyon Drive, in Hollywood, for a surprisingly low price. They didn't bother to inquire why the price was so low, or who had previously owned the place. They just considered themselves lucky and moved right in.

Then one night as they went up to their bedroom they discovered why the place had changed owners so many times and why more knowledgeable people had rejected the house, in spite of the very attractive price. Standing there, cape flapping in the non-existent breeze, was Superman! The image faded quickly, and the couple realized that they had just seen a ghost.

This ghost had nothing to do with the well-publicized 1993 "death" of Superman in the comics. This incident took place back in the early 1960s. And it didn't take the couple long to find out who the ghostly man of steel was, and why he was there.

The house had been owned by the actor George Reeves, who had for many years played Superman in a long-running 1950s television series. At the time he was thoroughly identified with the part. So much so, that many believed he had been "typecast," and once the series ended he had difficulty finding other work. Many actors have suffered that fate. What at first looked like a good job really destroyed their careers. Being identified with a part like Superman just made the problem worse. After all, how could an audience take an actor seriously in an ordinary part, if they kept thinking that he was Superman?

The house on Benedict Canyon Drive was not only where Reeves had lived, it was the house where he died under tragic and mysterious circumstances. Reeves's death remains the subject of Hollywood gossip to this day.

Others had seen the ghost of George Reeves in the house, but he was usually dressed in a bathrobe, rather than his familiar Superman costume. That was the reason the house had changed hands so many times and why the price was so low. The place was haunted.

Prior to his Superman role, George Reeves had been

a minor actor in a lot of minor films. His career seemed to be going nowhere. To tell the truth, George Reeves wasn't a very good actor. But he was square-jawed and muscular; he really looked a lot like the Superman of the comic books. While getting the part was really a big break, Reeves wasn't particularly happy with the role. He always thought he was capable of better things than the two-dimensional character of the greatest comic book superhero. And back in those days, when television was still in its infancy, the title role in a successful series did not necessarily make an actor rich. He was pretty well paid by the standards of the day, but he was usually spending more than he made. Perhaps that is why he stuck with "Superman" from 1951 to 1957, when the series finally ended.

The circumstances surrounding Reeves's death are puzzling and disturbing. As the "Superman" show was winding down, the actor broke up with his longtime girlfriend. He also began drinking heavily.

Then quite abruptly he announced that he was going to marry a showgirl whom he had only recently met. His friends thought the woman had rather sinister associates and that she encouraged his excessive drinking. Reeves also started getting strange and threatening phone calls, up to twenty or thirty of them a day. The rumor was that they were from his ex-girlfriend but no one knew for sure. Reeves wouldn't give details of what the calls were about.

On the night of June 15, 1959, Reeves's fiancée arranged a party at the Benedict Canyon house. The pair were due to fly to Mexico and be married in just a few days. Lots of people showed up, and were apparently having a good time. George Reeves, however, was not in a partying mood. He made a brief appearance and was dressed in his bathrobe. After a few minutes he went upstairs.

Then, according to the *Los Angeles Times*, his girl-friend announced to a group, "George is going to kill himself." There was a shot and everyone ran up to the bedrooms. George Reeves was sprawled across the bed, the still-smoking gun beside him.

The death was ruled a suicide, though there was no note. Reeves's mother couldn't accept that verdict and was convinced some sort of foul play was involved. She hired a well-known Hollywood private investigator to look into the circumstances. The investigation came to nothing.

The story was big news for a while. There was a lot of speculation as to why "Superman" killed himself. The popular theory was that he had become depressed when the series ended, because he had been so typecast that he was unable to find other work. He was certainly depressed, but the truth is he already had several other acting jobs lined up, and there was a good possibility that the "Superman" series was actually going to be renewed.

There was talk that the threatening phone calls from the ex-girlfriend drove Reeves to take his own life. Yet when his will was read, it was found that he left everything he owned to her.

In the end, the questions surrounding the death of George Reeves have never been adequately answered. In spite of this, and perhaps because of the mystery, the old Superman series has remained very popular. It is still regularly rerun throughout the country, and Reeves himself has become something of a cult hero to a whole new generation that had not even been born when the show first was aired. You might be able to catch an episode on one of the cable channels tonight. An autographed photo of Reeves as Superman sells for $2,000. It is one of the most prized and expensive TV star autographs.

And what of the ghost? Stories of the appearance of George Reeves, either with or without his Superman costume, continue to circulate on Benedict Canyon Drive.

CHAPTER ELEVEN

"The Table Wishes to Speak to You"

ONE OF THE MOST successful Broadway producers during the first half of the twentieth century was Guthrie McClintic. It was a time when Broadway producers were really important. McClintic had an almost unerring eye for picking hits. But he always attributed his success to a . . . Well, let's begin from the beginning.

Around 1913 Guthrie McClintic was one of the crowd of young aspiring actors who had been drawn to New York in search of a career in the theater. He was subsisting on a small allowance from his family in Seattle, and making the rounds of producers' offices looking for a part. In the previous year he had had exactly five weeks of work, and he was beginning to feel pretty low.

One day, while sitting on a bench in Bryant Park, he met another young actor whom he knew. The fellow informed him with great satisfaction that *he* had just been signed by the great producer, Winthrop Ames, for a role in his new play.

Figuring that if Ames had hired one unknown he might just be willing to hire another, McClintic rushed to the producer's office. There he was informed that "Mr. Ames was not seeing anyone." However, he could get an interview with Ames's assistant, George Foster Platt. Platt was a forbidding figure, who never failed to terrify young actors.

"After Platt had informed me, quite politely, that there was nothing in prospect for me, I continued to sit, fairly frozen in my chair. Finally, to terminate the interview, he thrust his hand across the table and said firmly, 'Good afternoon, Mr. McClintic.' "

The awed and frightened young man reached over the desk to shake hands, and in so doing, knocked over a fancy inkwell that stood on the desk. "I think that was the most horrible moment of my life, watching that pool of ink spreading over his papers. I tried to do something about it but Platt, by now in a cold rage, told me to go—to get out—and called his assistant."

At this point McClintic figured his career, if not his life, was just about over. But soon this sense of depression was replaced by a feeling of anger—anger at Winthrop Ames, whom he blamed for having refused to see him in the first place. Ames had the reputation of favoring mainly British actors. McClintic sat down and wrote a letter to Ames accusing him of letting talented young American actors starve, and telling him what he thought should be done in the theater.

McClintic recalls the letter "was a masterpiece of sorts." But by the time he had finished it, he cooled off a bit. He just put the letter in his pocket and went home. He then tossed the letter in a trunk and thought no more about it.

Five weeks later McClintic's employment prospects had not improved a bit. He was, as he said, moving from depression to desperation, and was thinking of getting a job as a messenger or an elevator operator. He couldn't bear to ask his family for more money because he knew he would get the inevitable "We told you so."

Then his landlady knocked at the door and said, "Mr. McClintic, the table wishes to speak to you."

To most people that would be a very strange and puzzling statement. But McClintic knew exactly what it meant. His landlady, Mrs. Henisohn, was a devotee of the practice known as "table tipping." She believed that she could communicate with the spirit world by means of a table-tipping code. "I remember hearing the table thumping away, many times far into the night, and I knew that Mrs. Henisohn was getting messages from some 'familiar,' usually a relative long since deceased, who addressed her as 'cousin Ada.'"

The code was a simple but crude one. When she wanted answers to a question, Mrs. Henisohn would slowly recite the alphabet aloud. When she reached a certain letter, the table, leaning back on two legs, would come down with a resounding thump. In this slow and laborious way messages would be spelled out.

So when his landlady made her strange statement, the young man did not need an additional explanation. He followed her down to the living room and sat by the table. At her instructions he began to chant the alphabet. Nothing happened until he reached the letter "M" and the table came down with a thud. He continued to go through the alphabet but nothing happened. He started again and at the very first letter, the table gave a thump. Slowly and meticulously the following message was sent:

MAILTHATWHICHYOUHAVEWRITTEN
YOURENTIREFUTUREDEPENDSUPONIT

Divided into words this read, *"Mail that which you have written, your entire future depends upon it."* That was the end of the message.

McClintic and his landlady were both surprised and disappointed by the message. They had been expecting something more dramatic. And they didn't have the faintest notion what the message was supposed to mean. Then suddenly McClintic remembered the letter he had written but never sent to Winthrop Ames. He had thrown it in his trunk and forgotten about it. He now felt sure that he must mail it. He assumed that he couldn't be hurt by it, because his position with Ames could be no worse than it already was.

The moment stuck in his mind. "By then it was well past midnight, but I dressed and set out to find the nearest letter box. I found it, I distinctly remember, at the corner of One hundred-fifteenth Street and Riverside Drive, and dropped the letter in. By now, it was two-thirty A.M. on this hot summer morning in June."

Within three days there was an answer, personally signed by Winthrop Ames. The producer said that the letter had interested him enormously, and he invited McClintic to come to his office. The young man was there the very next morning but was told Ames was not at work because he was ill. The following day Ames was still out of the office, and his secretary set an appointment for two days ahead. By this time McClintic was feeling as if the whole thing was some sort of terrible and cruel joke.

The third time Ames still wasn't there, but a contract was. He was offering to take McClintic on as an assistant stage manager for the sum of twenty-five dollars a week, an enormous salary for an unemployed actor. Ames had decided to employ the young man, sight unseen, on the strength of one angry letter.

McClintic worked for Ames for nine years, and became the producer's top assistant. He even worked in

George Foster Platt's old office, and at the same desk on which he had spilled the ink in 1913.

Ames helped him produce plays on his own, and he became very successful. McClintic lost touch with his old landlady, who had moved and left no forwarding address. But he did hear from her two more times. Once, he was planning to produce a play with a famous actress. When the plans were announced in the newspapers, he got a note from Mrs. Henisohn telling him to drop the project because the actress would never play the part. He ignored the warning. But the actress became seriously ill and had to leave the production. Rather than drop the show, the producer substituted another actress, but the play was a complete flop, one of the few real failures in his career.

McClintic heard from Mrs. Henisohn once more. He was producing a play called *The Barretts of Wimpole Street* that was to star his wife, the celebrated actress Katharine Cornell. He had a lot riding on the production but things were going very badly. So badly, he was on the verge of giving up the whole project when his secretary told him he had a telephone call from a woman who would identify herself only as "a friend" who had to talk to him on important business.

McClintic, who was already in a foul mood, exploded. He said that he didn't have time to talk to idiots who announced that they were his "friend." Then, suddenly, he changed his mind and took the call.

A familiar voice said, "Nothing to worry about. You are about to have your greatest success to date." And then the phone went dead. "I have never seen or heard from her since," says McClintic.

On the basis of the phone call, McClintic decided to continue with the project, and the voice turned out to be correct. *The Barretts of Wimpole Street* proved to be his greatest theatrical hit.

CHAPTER TWELVE

Did Houdini Return?

To say that the great magician Harry Houdini did not believe in ghosts would be to put the matter far too mildly. He spent a large part of the final years of his career exposing fraud in the practice known as spiritualism. Spiritualists believe that it is possible to communicate with the dead with the aid of specially gifted persons called "mediums." During sessions or séances with a medium, all sorts of remarkable things were supposed to happen. The medium might fall into a trance and begin speaking in what was said to be the voice of a person long dead. The ghost or spirit of the dead might actually appear at a séance. There were millions of people throughout the world who believed in, or at least were deeply interested in, these practices.

Houdini thought that most spiritualist séances were fraudulent. He said that all the remarkable phenomena that were produced during a séance were the result of trickery. It was the sort of trickery that "honest" magicians like himself used on stage all the time. The difference, said Houdini, was that the mediums claimed that there was no trickery involved—that what they were doing was real.

Houdini set out to prove it was all trickery. He went to séances conducted by some of the country's leading mediums, and caught them at their tricks. He gave lectures and demonstrations, explaining just what the mediums did. He wrote books and articles on the subject, and he was very effective. Houdini was ferocious and unrelenting. Whenever a medium made a claim, Houdini was right there to denounce it. He became the greatest enemy of the spiritualists, and he helped to bring the whole practice into disrepute.

Yet it was also said that Harry Houdini really did want to find a way of communicating with the dead, and that he was furious at all the frauds. He told his wife, Bess, that if he died before she did, he would try to send her a message from beyond, if such a thing were possible. He said that the message would be in a code that only the two of them knew, and that she should only pay attention to coded messages.

In 1926, while Houdini was on tour, he was backstage talking to some of his admirers. He told them that he was so well-conditioned and trained that he could be hit in the stomach and not feel the pain. He asked one of his listeners to hit him. The man, who was quite strong, did so. The blow was delivered so quickly that the magician did not have time to tense up his muscles and protect himself. He received internal injuries. This led to complications and on Halloween, 1926, Harry Houdini died.

Bess, who had seen her husband defy death in a thousand daring feats, could not accept what had happened. She had a complete breakdown, from which she never really recovered.

As you might expect, Bess was besieged by mediums who claimed that they were in contact with her dead husband. But none of them delivered any coded message.

On New Year's Day of 1929, Bess Houdini fell down a flight of stairs in her New York home. Before losing consciousness, she cried out, "Harry dear, why don't you come back to me from the other side." This incident was widely reported in the newspapers.

One week later she was contacted by a spirit medium named Arthur Ford. Ford said that in a séance he had received a message from Harry Houdini's mother. Houdini's mother, who had been dead for many years, had always been very close to her son, and the magician was deeply affected by her death. It was said that her death was what sparked Houdini's interest in the possibility of communicating with the dead in the first place. The message seemed interesting enough for Bess to arrange for a séance with Ford.

On January 8, 1930, Bess and several friends held the séance with Ford in the Houdini living room. During the séance this message was delivered: "Rosabelle, answer, tell, pray, answer, look, tell, answer, answer, tell."

It didn't seem to make any sense to anyone in the room except Bess. She became pale and nearly fainted. "Rosabelle" was a song that Bess, who had been her husband's stage assistant, had sung in their very first performance together. The first lines of the song were engraved on the inside of her wedding band. In a voice trembling with emotion, Bess sang:

> Rosabelle, sweet Rosabelle
> I love you more than I can tell.
> Over me you cast a spell
> I love you, my sweet Rosabelle.

Then she fainted.

The rest of the message was quickly decoded. It, too, dated back to the early days of the Houdini act, when the couple used a numbered-word code in a mind-reading act. When decoded the message consisted of one highly significant word: *Believe.*

News of Houdini's message from beyond created an immediate sensation. The archenemy of spiritualism seemed to have provided the ultimate evidence for the belief. Even today, over sixty years later, the Houdini message is often cited as proof of communication with the dead.

But is it really the ironclad proof that it appears to be at first? A closer look at the story of the Houdini message raises some serious problems. One of Houdini's fellow magicians, Joseph Dunninger, said the whole thing was a fraud. He pointed out that the "secret code" was no secret, that the solution to it had been printed in a biography of the magician just a year after his death.

Dunninger and other friends of Houdini did not believe, or at least did not say, that they thought Bess Houdini had taken part in the fraud. But one newspaper reporter claimed that he had actually heard Ford and Mrs. Houdini plotting the thing together. The reporter said that they planned to go on tour and make a lot of money, and they almost certainly would have. In any case, Bess was not a well woman. She had never really recovered from Houdini's death, and she had been drinking heavily. She retracted her statement that the communication had been genuine. Ford himself never actually said that the message was fake, but he had a long career as a spiritualist and he never talked about the Houdini message as much as he might have. He always seemed a bit nervous about it and didn't want to spend too much time explaining what had happened.

Some people even doubt whether Houdini ever really

had a plan to try to send back a message from the dead. He may have thought the whole idea was rather pointless.

Bess Houdini, however, did not give up trying to communicate with her dead husband. For many years on Halloween, the anniversary of Harry Houdini's death, she continued to hold séances. She still hoped that a genuine message would come through. Finally she gave up, discouraged. "When I go," she told a friend, "I'll be gone for good. I won't even try to come back."

Still every Halloween, spirit mediums throughout the world hold séances, and there are always a few who claim that they have received a message from Harry Houdini. That is as regular and predictable a part of Halloween as pumpkins and black cats.

CHAPTER THIRTEEN

The Ghost in the Machine

IT HAD TO HAPPEN. Computers are finally being haunted. There are now many stories of ghostly messages appearing mysteriously on computer screens. Back in the nineteenth century, spirits of the dead were supposed to laboriously tap out their messages in a crude code, send messages via the Ouija board or write them on slates. Now they can do it on a PC and have the advantages of spell-check as well.

One of the stranger computer ghost stories to come along involves a professional wrestler. Back in the 1940s and 1950s, a man named Maurice Tillet wrestled under the name The French Angel. Tillet's story was an unhappy one. He was born in France and while he was in his twenties, he developed the condition called acromegaly. It is a disease that causes uncontrollable bone growth, and the result is hideous deformity. That is what happened to Maurice Tillet.

He was an extremely intelligent, well-educated, and sensitive man, who could speak fourteen different languages. Yet because of his appearance, he was unable to get a regular job. The only course open to him was to display himself as some sort of a freak in the professional wrestling ring. He began wrestling in his native France but soon moved to America, where wrestling was far more popular and thus more lucrative. Under the name The French Angel, he became one of the ring's most popular attractions.

Another feature of acromegaly is that it shortens one's life span. Tillet died in 1955 at the age of forty-five.

During his lifetime, Tillet made many friends who were able to look beyond his deformities to see the real person underneath. He was neither a freak nor a monster.

One of the friends he made was an American businessman named Patrick Kelly. The two often played chess together. Tillet was an excellent player, who was familiar with all the intricacies as well as the history of the game. Kelly recalled that his friend often remarked, "How awful it is to be imprisoned in this body."

In 1980, a full twenty-five years after Tillet's death, Kelly bought an electronic, computerized chess game.

He kept the game on a desk in his library, where there was also a plaster cast of Maurice Tillet's death mask. A death mask is a plaster cast of the face of someone who has just died. Such items may seem gruesome souvenirs, but at one time they were very common, and not regarded as morbid in any way.

The chess-playing computer played a good, but very standard game. The computer doesn't make mistakes, but it doesn't make any innovative moves either. Late one evening Kelly was playing a game with the computer when it did something unusual. Instead of ordinary moves that were in the computer program, it used an eighteenth-century opening series of moves that had been favored by a famous French chess master. This was also a series that Tillet had often used. Kelly did not think too much about the change at first.

"I played out the game, and the next morning noticed that the computer was not plugged in. I thought nothing of it at the time, but a few weeks later the computer suddenly used a similar opening—and again it was not connected to any power supply."

Kelly says he found that the computer would operate without electricity only when it was placed near Tillet's death mask. The puzzled businessman had the mask X-rayed to see if it contained any electronic devices. It contained nothing.

The electronic chess set would not work all the time. Sometimes the unplugged set would be inactive for days or weeks. To Kelly, this indicated that Tillet's spirit was not present.

According to Kelly, "When I want a game, I set up the pieces without plugging the set in. If there is no response, then I know Maurice is elsewhere." Kelly might then plug the set in and begin to play. "Often in midgame the computer will play above its normal level, and I know he has stopped by. I prove this by pulling out the plug, but the game still goes on."

Kelly says that he is happy that his friend's spirit, finally released from the body that had become so burdensome, is still able to enjoy a good game of chess now and then.